MW01074450

Wild Surprises

Also by Carol Flake Chapman

Maybe We Will All Become Butterflies
Poems from the Pandemic

Written in Water
A Memoir of Love, Death and Mystery

Redemptorama
Culture, Politics and the New Evangelicalism

Tarnished Crown
The Quest for a Racetrack Champion

Thoroughbred Kingdoms
Breeding Farms of the American Racehorse

New Orleans
Behind the Masks of America's Most Exotic City

Wild Surprises

*Stories and Poems about
Encounters That Shifted My World*

*For my favorite
Ukrainian
composer*

Carol Flake Chapman

2nd Tier Publishing
Wimberley, Texas

Copyright © 2021 by Carol Flake Chapman

Published by 2nd Tier Publishing, Wimberley, Texas

All rights reserved. No part of this book may be used or
reproduced or transmitted in any form whatsoever without
written permission from the author, except for inclusion of
brief quotations in a review.

ISBN 978-1-7350664-4-8

Book design by Dan Gauthier

For my Dad,
who taught me that even snakes can be beautiful.

Contents

Contents

Acknowledgments

Portions of "The Eyes of the Gorilla" were previously published in the *Boston Globe Sunday Magazine.*

Portions of "Alydar's Ghost" were previously published in *Connoisseur Magazine.*

Portions of "The Winning Camel" were previously published in *The New Yorker Magazine.*

Portions of "A Butterfly Story, Part I: The Mysteries of Migration" were previously published in *Conde Nast Traveler Magazine.*

Portions of "The Wind Horse and the Mountain Snake" were previously published in *NextTribe* online magazine.

The poem "The New Extinction Math" was previously published in *Poets Reading the News* online magazine.

The poem "Sequestered Sunday" was previously published in my book *Maybe We Will All Become Butterflies: Poems from the Pandemic* and in the Proverse anthology *Mingled Voices 5.*

The poem "For Molly: A Dog" was previously published in *NextTribe* online magazine.

"The River That Masquerades as a Lake" was included in an anthology, *Texas Rivers*, published by the Wittliff Collection and Texas A&M University Press,

Introduction

Like so many of us, I've experienced unusual encounters over the years with animals and birds in the wild, the kind of encounters with beings from the natural world that don't fit into the ordinary scheme of things. More than simply coincidences, these wild surprises, as I've come to call them, point to a dimension of our world that is beyond our everyday understanding. From a Spanish dagger plant that asked for my help by falling gently on my shoulder to a young gorilla who gazed lovingly into my eyes in the highland jungle of Rwanda, these beings have startled me with their willingness and desire to connect, using their own way of communicating. It's as though they were speaking to me in a lost mother tongue, as my friend Will Taegel calls it, a language that I've only begun to learn: the deep, primal, but infinitely diverse language of earth-based relatedness.

Some of these encounters came during the course of my work as a journalist. And not all of them came while I was in the wild, but claimed my attention in unexpected places: a racing camel in the desert of Dubai, a noisy lizard in Bali, a swan on the lake near my home. Many of these experiences came after the sudden death of my husband, during a prolonged period of mourning, when I felt that nature was somehow bending towards me, opening a portal to a deeper connection, a kind of kinship with the natural world and its creatures. It's not that nature was singling me out to offer solace to one bereft human, but that in my grief, I was split open enough to perceive the unexpected—and unearned—gifts of grace that are there for all of us, once we awaken to them. What I was learning was that the deep hole in my heart caused by grief could be filled with wonder.

Those of you who have read my book *Written in Water: A Memoir of Love, Death and Mystery,* or those who have heard me talk about my pilgrimage of healing after my husband's death, know that "synchronicities" have played a big role in my journey. Sychronicity happens, as Carl Jung wrote, when events appear to be connected in a deep, mysterious and timely way that we can't explain using ordinary logic. Jung felt that one day we would understand those connections when we come to understand the larger context in which they occur. One day. But until then, what do we do? Maybe we just accept them as part of what Buddhists call ordinary magic. Or maybe just meaningful coincidences.

In my journey, those experiences of meaningful coincidence have most often involved the natural world. Owls, hawks, swans, spiders, butterflies, even snakes—they have all made timely appearances and become part of my story. And those kinds of resonant experiences haven't stopped. As those who have embarked on a pilgrimage or any kind of "conscious" journey know, the path never really ends. Though these stories and the poems that were inspired by them reflect past encounters, they also point to the path ahead.

1

The Screech Owl, the Snook and the Warbler

My dad wasn't like other dads when I was a kid growing up in swampy Lake Jackson, Texas. Though he was a doctor overseeing the health of workers at the local Dow Chemical plant, he always seemed more at home in the woods or on the water. Sure, most dads in our small town hunted and fished. But my dad had a connection to the natural world that went beyond guns and fishing rods to a deep knowledge and awareness that probably went all the way back to his Choctaw ancestry.

I loved our walks in the woods that began then just beyond the edge of our property on Oyster Creek, which was once part of the old Jackson sugar plantation. A self-taught naturalist, he knew every tree, every wildflower, every bird, and even every bug we encountered. It turned out too that he was a snake whisperer. One day we came upon a coiled copperhead, and in the blink of an eye Dad had caught it behind the head so that I could see its fangs and know to avoid the snake but not to fear it. And not to loathe it. Another day we found an old slave graveyard deep in the woods, which brought home what had once happened on the land long ago. We stopped and paid silent tribute. I didn't feel the site was haunted, but it was immeasurably sad. (The graveyard is now surrounded by the concrete parking lot of a large shopping mall.)

Living on Oyster Creek then seemed like an endless adventure. The creek was a muddy brown, and occasionally a huge alligator gar would roll, breaking the surface and showing only enough of itself to make me shudder. My neighbor Jay Dunn and I would take my dad's old rowboat out on the creek and pretend we were navigating the Amazon. Occasionally a water moccasin would slither by, reinforcing our fantasy.

We were surrounded by wild creatures, which sometimes made their way into our house. My dad was always rescuing injured or orphaned baby birds and animals, and they became part of the household. My favorite was Screechie the screech owl, who would fly from atop the curtains to land on our shoulders, where she would preen and peck our ears, making little cooing sounds. It was difficult to let her go, but she came back occasionally to perch on the patio outside the dining room window and peer in at us. And then there was Rocky the flying squirrel who would also make forays from the curtain rods to various points. But I had a special place in my heart for three baby possums that my dad found in the pouch of their dead mother and brought home. We named them Tom Dick and Blossom Possum, and I would carry one of them around in my purse, even taking it to school one day. We took all three camping with us to West Texas.

My dad was determined to make me a good fisherman, and he taught me how to catch grasshoppers and dig up worms for bait. It never occurred to me to be squeamish. He taught me how to take a slice of silvery fish skin and make it flutter through the water to attract the huge alligator gars that fed mostly at night. I wasn't sure I actually wanted to catch one, despite the challenge. One afternoon, though, while I was fishing by myself on the little wooden pier my dad built over the creek, I felt a powerful tug on the line and was horrified to see that I had actually snagged a gar, which looked to be about six feet in length, making it well over a foot longer than I was tall. I proceeded to engage in an hour-long battle to pull it onto the bank, where I gazed at it in fascinated horror, as tears of exhaustion coursed down my face.

I stopped fishing even before I went away to college, but a few years ago, I took my dad along on an assignment to write about Port Isabel, at the tip of South Padre Island on the Gulf Coast. As we drove south, with our fishing gear stashed in the trunk of my car, it felt like old times. It was late in the day when we finally headed for the jetties, where the waves were crashing, and I had second thoughts about this adventure. I pulled a thawed mullet from the bait bucket and secured it on the hook, following my dad's instructions, since I had forgotten nearly everything. My first cast went high, then fizzled, like a kid's first softball throw. My line nearly got snagged on the jetties. But on the next try, almost as soon as the mullet hit the water, I felt something really fighting on the end of the line. I reeled in a glimmering silver fish with a gold stripe and aggressive underslung jaw. I had never seen a fish like this.

"It's a snook," my dad said wonderingly. "Some people never catch a snook, ever." For the brief second or two as I admired my prized sporting fish, before releasing it back into the water, I felt as though I'd found South Padre's long-lost treasure. "Look," my dad said, and I glanced up at the last rays of the sun pouring through a round opening in the clouds, like the visions of heaven depicted on the interior of church domes we'd seen on a trip we took together in Italy.

My dad stopped hunting a long time ago. He bought the land in the Hill Country he had once used as a deer lease and built a cabin on it, where he has painstakingly catalogued every single wildflower, well over a hundred, that he has found blooming on the property. It's a magical place, perched on the edge of a canyon, and it is the kind of habitat preferred by the endangered golden cheek warbler. One day my late husband and I were sitting with my dad on the back porch of the cabin, and I asked my dad about the warblers. "Have you ever seen a golden-cheeked warbler?" he asked. "No," we replied. And just then a dark bird with bright gold cheeks and a white breast flew by and landed on a branch less than twenty feet where we were sitting. "Well, there's one," said my dad.

And that's how it goes when you are in tune with the wild.

The Things They Left Behind

The storm approaches in flashes of light
And distant thunder over the Devil's Backbone
Riffling the wind chimes that I gave them last year
Tubes tinkling random notes of Amazing Grace
As I stand on the back porch of the cabin

My dad bought the land as a hunter
And left it as a steward of the deer
And the wild turkeys, as a chronicler of wild flowers
A caretaker of the springs at the bottom of the canyon
That he swore would never go dry, but did last summer

Cold rain and sadness drive me inside
And I start a random inventory
Of things just starting to gather dust
So many of them souvenirs of random walks
Down the steep trail to the canyon floor

On the mantle, the improbable possum teeth gleam
Next to dry rattles from a snake reluctantly killed
After lurking under the cabin with children around
Fossilized shells proclaim the waves of an ancient sea
While flints and arrowheads speak of a vanished people

In a drawer are the scraps of cloth for a quilt never made
On a shelf are books never opened, some read twice
In the closet are shirts and jackets for a colder age
On a bureau sits a forgotten spritzer of Windsong perfume
Like a bottle of booze with maybe a swallow at bottom

They have left no fossils or carvings to intrigue scholars
But oh, out on the hillside where the air is clear
I can sense the living bounty of their presence here
Seeds sown into a blanket of bluebonnets greet me
And the old Christmas pine drops its cones like grenades

2

The Eyes of the Gorilla

*M*any years ago, when I was living in Boston, I got an invitation I couldn't refuse. A friend who was involved in animal rescue causes had been asked to participate in the world's first international gorilla festival in Rwanda, and she asked me to join her as a journalist. It had been almost five years since Dian Fossey, the fabled protector of the endangered mountain gorillas, had been murdered, and the small remnant of Rwanda's population of the reclusive primates she had made famous was still hanging on in the wild and tangled slopes of the once volcanic Virungas. It would be another four years before half a million of Rwanda's Tutsi people would be murdered in a genocidal attack, leaving the fate of the gorillas deep in the shadows.

As it turned out, the festival's organizer, a smooth operator from Ghana, who had promised that celebrities like Michael Jackson would attend, had absconded with most of the fundraising money by the time we arrived in the capital of Kigali. But the local supporters of the festival decided the show should go on, though the attendees would be mostly local people. We gathered in the capital's new Chinese-built soccer stadium for the opening festivities, which included the unveiling of a giant sculpture of a gorilla carved out of soap by an artist from the Pygmy Twa tribe—the contribution of the local Sulfo Soap company. Sulfo employees wearing T-shirts embossed with a picture of a baby gorilla and the slogan "Protegez-moi" (protect me) posed in front of the soap statue and passed out pamphlets containing an astonishly eloquent speech purported to be composed by a mountain gorilla:

"We see in each of you a Dian Fossey," said the anonymous gorilla, "and feel that our only solace and hope lies in good people like you. Hence we would request you…the entire brethren of the world (forgive us if we are wrong but we believe in Darwin's theory) to help us survive."

This spectacle was as moving as it was surreal, and most of us in our group of 60 or so, many of whom were from zoos, were in tears by the end of the ceremony. Among other things, we had learned that almost none of the local people who attended had actually ever seen a gorilla. As children, they had heard rumors and scary stories of the giant beasts high up in the mountains who were to be avoided. But local businesses who had put together booths and displays for the festival went to imaginative lengths to create a friendly image for the gorillas. At a popular refreshment stand sponsored by the Kigali Nightclub, patrons posed at tables in front of a mural depicting a suave-looking gorilla smoking a cigarette. A few booths down, owners of a shop called La Rotonde were selling a drawing of President Juvenal Habyarimana arm-wrestling with a gorilla and another of Dian Fossey and a gorilla with its arm around a photographer.

We learned that actually seeing the gorillas in Rwanda had already become a luxury that most Rwandans couldn't afford. Tourists, who were limited to a handful a day, were paying $120 for the privilege of going up to see the animals. Local people were given a lower rate, but very few actually took advantage of the opportunity.

Though most of us in our group had hoped to be able to view the gorillas, it turned out that only two of us were going to be able to go. In a very odd selection system, those who most wanted to go gave speeches, and the group voted on the candidates. As it turned out, I was chosen along with an African American photographer from Dallas. We were assigned to visit the family of gorillas known as Group 9, actually the most elusive and peripatetic of the four groups that had been "habit-uated," that is, accustomed to human visitors. This group was known to disappear often into what was then called Zaire (now known as the Democratic Republic of the Congo), where visitors were forbidden to follow. And so seeing them was not a sure thing.

We were assigned trackers from local villages, who carried ri-fles—not to use on the gorillas, we were assured, but to ward off irascible

Cape buffalos, which were learned were one of the greatest dangers in the jungle. Our guide was a veterinarian named Jean Bosco, who wore a bright red sweater that the gorillas had come to recognize. As a child, he said, he didn't know anything about the gorillas. But now, he said, the fate of the gorillas was tied up with that of the country. "Rwandans take the gorillas very seriously. If something happens to them, we will not survive." Surprisingly, he said, "there are many daughters in Rwanda named Dian so that they will be as brave and serious as Dian Fossey."

We set out through a towering stand of bamboo, which creaked eerily as the wind rubbed the stalks together. As we began to climb, the thin air was a shock. After a half hour, we came to an open meadow, dotted with gnarled hagenia trees and bright yellow blossoms of hypericum, with a vista of the volcano Visoke in the distance. After another half-hour came a zone of nasty nettles and densely tangled brush and vines. Then after two more hours of exhausting climbing, the trackers found the nests used by the Group 9 gorillas the night before.

After another hour of false leads, the trackers located the group, which we could hear before we could see them. There were sounds of loud chomping, and a tracker pushed back a branch to reveal a young female gorilla absorbed in munching a stick of bamboo like wild celery. It was though a curtain had opened on a play, with the foliage acting as the convention of the fourth wall. She appeared to ignore her audience, but suddenly she pushed the branch that the tracker was holding down even further and held it there as she continued to eat with the other hand. She appeared to enjoy being center stage.

Nearby, a huge silverback was sitting under a bush. With his round belly hanging over his legs, he was ensconced like a benevolent Buddha. But even without the echoes of King Kong, there is something remote and mysterious about a silverback, with his volcano-shaped head and massive, leathery torso. Chimpanzees are closer to us genetically, and gorillas, who branched off from the evolutionary tree that led to sapiens sooner than did the chimpanzee, suggest more emphatically the road not taken.

My attention, however, was drawn away from the paunchy silverback to a young blackback with a scar on his face, an adolescent named Kwabili, who was clearly the show-off of the family. Leaning back against a bush, he pulled his little sister into his lap and played with her like a doll. He gave her a bear hug, then placed his hand on her head and gazed solicitously into her eyes. After a moment, he thumped his chest lightly and playfully shoved her away. Finding a tracker in his path, he whirled his arms like a windmill until the tracker backed away. Then he joined his brother, who appeared close to the same size, and the two sat facing each other, patty-cake style, grooming each other's bellies. Kwabili bit his brother's foot playfully and growled softly, initiating a wrestling match. They hugged each other first and then began every arm and headlock known to crooked wrestlers. Kwabili then hugged his brother from behind and they sat together, nestled like spoons.

After a few moments Kwabili moved off to sit quietly by himself, his belly hanging over his stubby little back legs. He looked so huggable. I had been told by Jean Bosco not to look the gorillas in the eye, as that would be taken as a challenge. But I glanced at the tracker who was nearby, and he nodded, as though he knew I was asking permission. I sat down next to Kwabili, being careful not to look at him. But I simply couldn't help myself. I began turning my head toward him, ever so slowly, as he was doing the same. We were like two shy teenagers who were full of curiosity about each other. And then I was looking into his round reddish-brown eyes that were indescribably warm and, well, I have to say, loving. I felt as though I was looking into his soul, without barriers.

I knew just how Dian Fossey felt when she first met the gaze of the young gorilla Peanuts, who was the first of the wild gorillas she was studying to accept her. "The expression in his eyes was unfathomable. Spellbound, I returned his gaze—a gaze that seemed to combine elements of inquiry and acceptance." It was a gaze that would change her life forever, turning her from scientist to fierce protector.

Something happened to me that day as well, though I haven't returned to the Virungas. I don't know about Kwabili, but I was never the same after our encounter. He had opened a portal for me into the deep and eternal soul of the wild that has remained open to this day.

To Touch the Wild

What is it about the human touch
That can turn a Moray eel into a puppy
Twisting so its belly can be rubbed

What a gift we have of hands
That can caress so easily
That can find the spot that itches

What is it about the human voice
That can whisper in a horse's ear
As its eyes close halfway, listening

What a gift we have of talking
And singing and adoring in words
And sometimes in melodies

What is it about human longing
To connect with the wild so
Intimately that we must touch it

What a gift we have of this urge
To bridge the gap between worlds
With words and touch and love

And what is it about the wild
That longs for our touch
In ways that it has never known

What a gift for us all
That we can put away fear
For the moment and behold each other

It must be that we are meant
To greet each other in this way
To find what we didn't know we needed

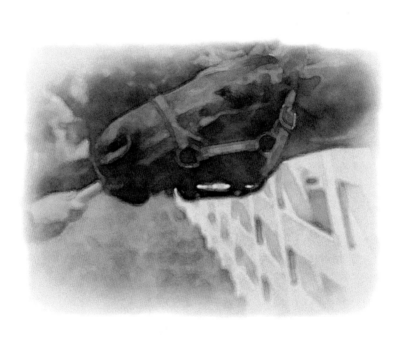

3

Alydar's Ghost

I didn't get to witness the epic Triple Crown duels in 1978 between the fabled thoroughbreds Affirmed and Alydar, all three of which were barely won at the wire by Affirmed. Those head-and-head duels are regarded as among the greatest in racing history. But I did get to see both horses eleven years later in their paddocks at Calumet Farm in Kentucky, where they were competing in a different kind of duel that Alydar was winning ably: as stallions at stud. At the time, Alydar, who was insured for $26 million, was the most valuable stallion in the world. I got to feed him a carrot, and I found him quite peaceable as stallions go. He was a really gorgeous horse with lots of personality, and I felt that I had gotten to meet a legend. I was writing a book at the time called *Thoroughbred Kingdoms*, about the history of America's great thoroughbred farms, of which Calumet was probably the most famous.

A year later I was back at Calumet under much different circumstances. Alydar had been euthanized after being discovered in his stall with a badly broken leg, supposedly after kicking his stall door, and Calumet had declared bankruptcy. I was there with an assignment from *Connoisseur Magazine* to write essentially a business story about how the most iconic thoroughbred farm had fallen into ruin so quickly and disastrously. Beautiful Calumet, jewel of the Bluegrass, breeder of more champions than any other American farm, had become under its president J.T. Lundy the center of a web of labyrinthine partnerships and soured business deals that reached across the country and around the world. Calumet had become, in the words of Alydar's former trainer John Veitch, a "house of cards," and within days of Alydar's death it had begun to crumble.

The first thing I wanted to do when I arrived at the farm on a hot summer day was to visit Alydar's stall. I wanted to see for myself where he had died, as it was so hard for me to imagine that such a vital being was gone. As it happened, I was accompanied on my tour of the farm by a burly, blond-haired young man named Alton Stone who said he had been Alydar's groom. He had been on temporary duty as a night watchman when Alydar was discovered in distress.

Alydar's nameplate was still displayed beside his stall, and as Alton opened the gate, his demeanor changed. We stood there in silence, and he began to weep. And as the hairs on the back of my neck began to tingle, I felt the presence of the great stallion. I knew then that what had happened to him was no accident. Something terrible had happened in that stall, and it was a different story from the one that had been told to Alydar's insurers. After working with thoroughbreds for a year at the racetrack, as I researched my first book on horse racing, I couldn't envision how or why Alydar would have kicked his stall door in the middle of the night hard enough to break the strongest bone in his body. Horses just don't kick like that, I thought. But the idea of foul play made no sense at the time, as Alydar, with his sky-high stud fees, was the bread and butter for the farm, whose finances were already beginning to unravel. I put away my suspicions for the time being. But I knew there was a mystery there that had to be solved, or Alydar's death was going to haunt me.

As I delved into the recent history of the farm as well as the records that were becoming available during the farm's bankruptcy proceedings, I discovered to my astonishment that Alydar was actually worth far more dead than alive. Though his breeding fees were as high as $100,000, J.T. Lundy had already sold lifetime breeding rights to a number of owners, and the stallion had been essentially overbooked for the next breeding season. There was no way the stallion, however randy he might be, could have "covered" the number of mares he had been booked to, with the fees already paid. What's more, I learned that one of the horse's major insurers had informed Lundy that the stallion would no longer be insured after the month of November—just two weeks before he was killed.

So there was a financial motive involved in Alydar's death. Insurance money. But the growing physical evidence I was uncovering was also pointing to suspicious circumstances. I felt as though Alydar was looking over my shoulder as I continued to try to figure out what had actually happened the night of his injury. When I saw the x-rays of the broken leg, which indicated a spiral fracture, I contacted a physics professor I knew who had made a study of thoroughbred motion. After careful study of the circumstances of Alydar's so-called accident, he concluded the injuries could not have resulted from a kick to the stall door. The injury, he said, had to have come from some kind of external force, perhaps even tying the leg to a moving vehicle.

The article I wrote for *Connoisseur* was titled "The Killing Fields," and though it caused quite a stir at the time in horse country, it looked as though J.T. Lundy was going to get away with, at the minimum, insurance fraud. But almost four years later I got a call from an FBI agent, who said that I had been correct in my conclusions that Alydar's death was not an accident, and he asked for my help in putting together a case, along with a young assistant attorney in Houston who was looking into it from the point of view of a corrupt banker there who had been involved in the farm's finances. As a result, I was able to explain some of the mysteries of the horse business and help them put together a paper trail, bringing in as well the analysis by the physics expert I had consulted. And I also served as an expert witness, including testimony from a conversation I had with Alton Stone when I visited him on impulse late at night as he was working on a job he taken at another farm. "J.T. knew something was going to happen to the horse," he told me.

It ultimately took ten years for all of this to result in justice for the horse who was known at the racetrack for never giving up. And so it is that when I think of Alydar, I am filled with sadness at what happened to him. But I also feel grateful for what I feel was his guidance as I helped to jail his killers.

What We Owe the Horses

They say you can hear the horses crying
In Palo Duro Canyon where they were shot
As the bullets killed the spirit of the Comanches

The white cavalrymen mourned their loss
As a horseman is a horseman no matter the color
And they shuddered at the wounds and the dying

Though we have mostly lost our connection
To horses there are children who remember them
From dreams long before they see a real one

They can hear them galloping on the plain
Snorting as their hooves thunder on
Beckoning them in a promise of freedom

They vanish in a cloud of dust like an old movie
Like the buffalo too that once rumbled there
So many they could not even be counted

They were once everything to us
Prancing before us in our carriages
Harnessed dutifully to our wagons

Carrying us on their backs
Or in front of us pulling a plough
Their ears flicking back and forth

They were collateral damage in wars
They took bullets for us and kept going
On the racetrack they gave us their hearts

So how can we thank them for all they've given
We can at least remember and let our souls
Run free with them on the wild and fenceless plain

4

The Winning Camel

The first time I saw a photograph of Mahna, a champion racing camel belonging to Sheik Mohammed Bin Rashid al Maktoum, the defense minister of Dubai, I thought the photo must have been tampered with. Mahna looked more like a surrealist's rendering of a greyhound than a camel. She had been photographed in full gallop as she crossed the finish line of the Nad al Shiba Racetrack in Dubai. Her long, curved neck and slender legs were stretched out from her elongated torso. On her back, clinging to her slightest of humps with one hand and raising a whip triumphantly with the other, was a boy dressed in purple and white racing silks.

I didn't know much about camels at the time, as I was immersed in the thoroughbred horse world as a racing correspondent for the New Yorker, but this image of a camel straining like a thoroughbred, giving her all at the finish line, caused me to reconsider my preconceptions about camels. And about camel racing. There is a certain goofiness, it must be admitted, to the appearance of the camel, what with its big, long-lashed eyes, its flappy, prehensile harelip, its round teddy-bear ears and its nose always in the air. Camels have an endearing way of looking noble and silly at the same time. But Mahna, with her swift racing gallop, was a different kind of animal, I suspected, and she was offering an unexpected path for me to follow — into the rapidly changing world of the desert sheikdoms of the Persian Gulf.

Dubai had become a place of mirages and illusions, where former Bedouin nomads drive Range Rovers, and the children of sheiks skate on ice rinks in shopping complexes copied from Houston. Yet amid this shifting and somewhat schizophrenic environment, camels and camel racing had become nostalgic symbols for the vanishing nomadic life. Although Bedouins have been racing camels in the desert for centuries, organized camel racing, with fences, grandstands and annual race meetings was a recent phenomenon, promoted in large part by Sheikh Mohammed, who had already begun to make his mark in thoroughbred horse racing in Europe and the U.S., paying eye-popping prices for top yearlings at auction and beginning to win big races.

When I arrived in Dubai, one of my first stops was to the camel backstretch near the racetrack to visit Mahna, who was being pampered by attendants who were brushing her already gleaming reddish-gold coat. I had quickly gotten to know Sheikh Mohammed's chief camel veterinarian Ahmed Billah, from Pakistan, who told me that Mahna was set to compete in the Gold Cup, the biggest race of the annual camel racing meet in which top racing camels from around the Persian Gulf, particularly from the Emirates, were entered. Mahna, who was now seven years old, was undefeated in five years of racing. "Mahna was bred by Sheik Mohammed," said Dr. Billah, "and she is his special camel." I was surprised to learn that only female camels, which were acknowledged as superior to males in racing ability, were allowed in the Gold Cup. We set out in his Range Rover on a paved road parallel to the main racetrack, where trainers actually drove during the races, egging on their young jockeys via walkie talkies. Even Sheikh Mohammed, he said, would be out in his Ranger Rover during a race to direct his jockey.

With the Gold Cup a week away, I had time in the afternoons to watch the camel races that were broadcast on TV from the oasis of Al Ain, and I found myself getting addicted. The races were accompanied by recordings of old Bedouin camel songs known as tagruds, which were marching songs traditionally used to pace the camels on a long journey over the desert. It was not unusual for men to sing to their camels. On the camel backstretch, I even saw a trainer kiss his camel on the snout. What's more, I learned, camels that distinguished themselves in the races were honored by "kaseedas," or poems of praise, a custom dating back for centuries. At the conclusion of the race, the Bedouin poet would come forward to recite a paean to the victorious camel, reflecting on its glorious ancestry and the honor of its owner. As a poetic form, the kaseeda had originally been composed on camelback, and its meter reflected the rocking pace of the camel.

As the week went on, I began to develop the harebrained idea of about writing a kaseeda myself. I hadn't written a poem since graduate school, but something about the camels and their soothing, rocking rhythm was inspiring. And of course, if I was to write about a winning camel, what better subject than Mahna? And so I began to write a poem with the rocking, lulling rhythm of the camel races in my head, along with the image of the camel as the ship of the desert. I loved the dhows, the small trading ships of the region, and the combination of camels and boats kept me thinking of the line from Walt Whitman, "Out of the cradle endlessly rocking," with its image of the ocean and its tidal rhythms. I presented the resulting effort to Dr. Billah, who only half-jokingly suggested that if Mahna should win the big race the following week, I ought to read the poem aloud to the assembled spectators. "That would be a first," he said. Though Islam does not allow gambling on races, I felt that I would be placing a kind of bet on Mahna. My words would be my wager.

On the day of the races, the tension and excitement had begun to build, as sheikhs and various dignitaries from around the region began to arrive. Around the track, there were guards everywhere, carrying machine guns, and a huge military helicopter was parked in front of the majlis (meeting hall) across the way. The Gold Cup would be the last race of the day, following a card of preliminary races. The ceremonies would get underway once the guest of honor, Sheikh Zayed of Abu Dhabi, head of the United Arab Emirates, arrived by limousine. A military band marched onto the track, and they launched into the national anthem of the UAE as Sheikh Zayed entered the grandstand with an entourage. He and the other sheikhs in attendance made their way to a private enclosure in the grandstand, while the rest of the crowd filled the stands.

I sat down next to a team of advisers to Sheikh Khalifa of Abu Dhabi that was led by an Australian named Heath Harris, who had trained horses for the films Pharlap and Breaker Morant, two of my favorites. During a trip to Abu Dhabi, Harris had applied an old horse trainer's trick to a camel with the annoying habit of sitting down during the race (he never explained his secret method), and Sheikh Khalifa had hired him on the spot. Harris said that he expected their team's top camel, Misiah, to give Mahna a run for the money.

As the camels entered the track, I could see Mahna, her reddish coat gleaming, among 18 other camels from around the Gulf. A racing official fired a starting pistol, and the cord serving as the starting gate whizzed back into its housing. The camels broke in a bunch. A camel owned by Sheikh Tahnoon took the lead. Mahna was in fourth position, moving steadily up along the rail, and in a flash, she had taken the lead. She was gliding along fluidly, her action effortless by comparison to the animals bounding along behind her. Misiah, however, was right at her heels, pressing her all the way. This was shaping up like a real duel. I wondered if Mahna would be able to keep up such a blazing pace. Her jockey had not yet even flexed his whip. Finally, as she neared the home-stretch, she began to edge away from Misiah. There was a tremendous roar as she came into sight at the top of the stretch, her lead increasing with every stride. She was going to set a new track record, covering the 10 kilometers at Nad al Shiba in under 18 minutes. It was as an amazing a performance as I had ever seen in a top thoroughbred race. In the old days of the desert, I thought, epic poems about Mahna would have been recited around the campfire.

Swept up in the drama of the moment, I walked over to one of Sheikh Mohammed's guards and told him I had a poem I wanted to read in Mahna's honor. He raised his eyebrows incredulously, but went off to the sheikhs' enclosure. In a moment, a tall, elegant man from Sheikh Mohammed's entourage emerged. "Now what is this about a poem?" he inquired. I explained that I had written a poem about Mahna. He went back inside to call Sheikh Mohammed, who was still on the track in his Range Rover. A moment later, he came back out, followed by Sheikh Mohammed's chief bodyguard. "Come with us," he said, and led me down to the lawn in front of the grandstand. The bodyguard then led me across the track, and we walked inside the control room where the television director, wearing headphones, was seated in front of a dozen TV screens. The race had been telecast all across the Persian Gulf, and the broadcast was wrapping up.

The bodyguard spoke to the director, who then shouted angrily, and practically yanked out his hair at this unexpected glitch in the broadcast schedule. After a moment, he calmed down and told us to go outside to find the race announcer, who then handed me his microphone. He aimed me toward a TV camera, and after offering a salutation to the visiting dignitaries as he had recommended, I read my poem. I could hear my voice booming out across the track, as I concluded, "Where her forerunners once roamed without roads, she shares with her master not merely the gift of survival but the will to win." When I was finished, I was surprised to hear thunderous applause coming from the grandstand. Soon I was surrounded by Bedouin trainers, who smiled warmly and pantomimed talking into the microphone. Though many did not understand English, they knew a poem when they heard one.

My poem was published the next day in the Gulf News of Dubai along with a description of Mahna's victory. And two days later, as I was packing up reluctantly to leave Dubai, Dr. Billah called and said to wait for him, as he was coming to pick me up. He had a surprise for me, he said. Or at least Sheikh Mohammed did. And so we headed to what I learned was the sheikh's sports palace, one of his many palaces, where I sat down on a low couch next to Dr. Billah and was served a fruit drink. Sheikh Mohammed arrived with his young son Ahmed and sat down across from me with a smile. We talked horses and camels for a bit. His strategy for the race, he said, had been simply to let her "run the other camels into the ground. She wants to win," he said. "Instead of fighting her, let her do it for herself. She is intelligent, and she keeps her energy for the right time. She knew she would do it in her own way."

He then held out a small black box, which I opened with trepidation. It was a medallion with a camel on one side and the engraved name Mahna on the other. "So you will not forget her," he said. And how could I ever forget the magical red-gold camel whose speed and heart taught me a lesson about a culture far different from mine and inspired me to begin writing poetry again, though I have yet to write another kaseeda.

In Praise of Mahna

If the dhow is born
From the foam of the sea
The camel, the dhow of the desert
Is born from the earth
Lending shape and purpose
To shifting sands.

Out of the desert she sails,
Endlessly rocking
Soothing as a lullaby,
Solid as a stone
Fast as a falcon,
Mahna, the wonder of Dubai.

In her stride are eons of journeys
From oasis to oasis
From camp to camp
Where her ancestors
Roamed without roads.
And now she shares
With her master not merely
The gift of survival
But also the will to win.

5

The Lizard in Paradise

M any many years ago, despite all my travels to exotic places, I had never been to Bali, one of the fabled places in my imagination, and I convinced my husband Gary to tag along with me on an exploratory trip for the travel company I was working for at the time. The island had been through a terrible financial slump, along with terrorist attacks on its sybaritic beach discos that dampened the tourist trade, and the government was encouraging visitors. Because of its devalued currency, everything was incredibly cheap, embarrassingly so for someone visiting from a prosperous country. When we exchanged our dollars fat the airport when we arrived, we almost looked for a wheelbarrow to carry the wads and wads of bills that poured out of the ATM machine. This was not what I expected for one of the most beautiful places on earth.

I had rented a car, though what was wheeled out for me at the rental agency at the airport was not exactly what you'd expect, even from a stripped down dune buggy. There was essentially no back cushion for the driver's side, so it was like sitting on a stool behind the steering wheel. Worse still, driving was on the left side of the road, British-style, and I had a heck of a time changing gears using my left hand, coaxing the vehicle's reluctant, primitive stick shift, meanwhile dodging trucks and chickens in the road. Doing all of this at once required intense concentration.

So off we set, but before we had gone ten miles, a vehicle with some sort of official insignia motioned us to stop. We later learned it was a mistake to stop, and we should have just kept going. The language barrier kept us from understanding what we had done wrong, but my husband grabbed a wad of bills and thrust it at the official, who accepted it and waved us on. As we later figured it out, we had given him a bribe of about 3 American dollars.

I had reserved us a bungalow in a once famous but slightly down-on-its-luck hotel near the town of Ubud. The hotel, with its bungalows cascading down a hillside overlooking a field of waving green elephant grass, had been the home of an expat who apparently liked erotic sculptures, as the place was adorned with monkeys in various suggestive poses that were arrayed around the pool. Every morning, the sculptures were adorned with bright red blossoms, as were the small shrines that we saw everywhere.

Despite the strange odors wafting from the hotel's antiquated septic system, we felt we had indeed arrived in paradise that had been emptied of tourists. We could hear the sepulchral tones of the gamelan and smell the burning sandalwood from the many ceremonies taking place around us in the evenings, as the local people seemed to be suspended in some sacred quotidian that honored the passage of life as part of a divine pattern. I still pine for the smell of sandalwood after all this time.

The problem came in the wee hours of the morning, when we began hearing a loud, disturbing noise coming from somewhere inside the bungalow. I began to time it, and the noises were coming every 30 minutes after about 3am. It sounded like something was screaming a name, followed by a downward trill. The name was something like Toe-kay, as broadcast shrilly through a megaphone. Finally I had enough, and I pinpointed the noise coming from behind a tall bureau. But what the heck was it making that godawful noise? I had to know.

I walked down from our bungalow to a kind of marshy area with bulrushes and elephant grass, where I cut a long branch with leaves, which I thought would work to scare whatever was making the noise out from behind the bureau.

That night I waited up until I heard the noise, but decided I should wait a little longer until there was enough light to see whatever it was that emerged. And so when the noise started again at dawn I swept the branch behind the bureau, and lo and behold, what emerged was something out of myth: a big blue lizard with gold spots. I had never seen anything like it. I actually love lizards and I'm not afraid of them, but this was by far the biggest and gaudiest one I had ever seen.

I chased this little dragon around the bungalow until it ran into the bathroom. As it was scrambling around in the slippery bathtub, I grabbed it behind the neck, as I had learned from my dad so many moons ago about safely catching a snake or lizard. It was about a foot and half long, and it opened its mouth, as though to bite. I hoped it wasn't poisonous, though it didn't seem to have fangs. I carried it outside the bungalow and carefully let it go. Finally we'd get some sleep.

Nope. The lizard was back that night. Toe-kayyyyyy. No sleep. So the next morning I went to the hotel concierge and explained that we had a problem with a lizard keeping us up at night. "Oh, but he is a lucky animal," said the concierge. I was sure he had in mind the small geckos that were lodged on the ceiling of the bungalow and chirped occasionally.

"Come with us," I said, and he followed us to the bungalow. I took the trusty branch with leaves and swept it behind the bureau. Out scampered the turquoise lizard, gripping the wall with its sucker-like toes, and the concierge gasped in astonishment. His mouth hung open, and his eyes were like saucers, so I gathered this was not a regular occurrence at the hotel. The lizard dodged into the bathroom, and I caught him again, this time using a towel. And this time the creature didn't really resist, as though we had created a kind of routine. He seemed resigned to his fate.

"What should I do with him," I asked the concierge, who suggested with a smile that I might let him go in the adjacent bungalow. I looked down at the bejeweled creature I had captured, this time really looking at him. He was really so beautiful if so annoying. He was a spectacular version of the little geckos I had around my house back home, and so this time when I let him go, it was with a certain reluctance. And he didn't return.

I learned when I returned home to my computer that our speckled turquoise intruder was a Tokay gecko, actually named for the loud sounds it makes. Though beautiful, it was not recommended as a pet, as it was known to bite rather viciously. But I had held this beautiful creature from the wild in my hands, and of all the wonders of Bali, this was the one I would remember most.

Inside Out

You can't keep them out these emissaries
Bearing messages from beyond our ken
Last night it was the fluttering that startled me
From my futile attempts to clear my desk
Of clutter from unpaid bills and piles of guilt
As a chimney swift battered her wings again
And again against the skylight that trapped her
In the illusion of escape to the brightness above

And then she found her way to a butterfly mask
I had made long ago while in a redwood forest
As though perhaps those wings would take her
Away from this stifling confusing prison indoors

This morning I woke up and went to the door
And looked out through the panes of glass
That had fogged over in the humid air
To see they had become tablets written upon
By a tiny snail who had left a clear trail
Behind him in his complicated wandering
So that I was looking out into the world
Through a pattern that appeared random

But probably not so to the busy snail
Who had created his own labyrinth
An agonizingly slow vaporous whorling
That was his signature for me to decode

6

The Grackle's Gift

I've always been ambivalent about grackles. They remind me of the dinosaur origins of birds, and it's not hard to imagine a grackle as a prehistoric raptor. They can be annoying when they congregate en masse on trees, where cars parked below are soon covered in their leavings. I even fancied myself a grackle whisperer, or more accurately a grackle shouter, as I managed to shoo them away from my backyard by yelling at them, "Bad grackle!" and chunking small rocks at them. For some reason, they listened and left my yard alone. They haven't been back, as perhaps my reputation has lingered. But they're fascinating in their own way, and when the sunlight shines on them in a certain way, they glisten. I'd actually like to make friends, if I could do so without all the droppings.

One Sunday afternoon at my local H-E-B grocery store, I took my basketful of goodies to the 15-items-or-less counter to check out. I actually had 16 items, as I laid them out on the moving counter, but I thought this was not an egregious crime, as grocery overloading goes. But there was an older man behind me, who was fuming. I could hear some indignant snorting. But I ignored him, as he was dressed in a ludicrous combination of Bermuda shorts and crisp white shirt with some sort of nautical insignia on it, finished off by ankle-high socks and some sort of boat shoes. I placed my bag in a cart and wheeled it out to my car. As I was about to unload the bag, I saw that the man in the Bermuda shorts had followed me. Closely. Every step of the way.

"You had too many items," he shouted, and I could see the spit fly through the air.

I was flabbergasted, frankly, and in those situations, words just come out of my mouth unbidden. Not always to a good result. But I had been to church that morning, vowing to work on my temper and to learn to turn the other cheek. And so the words that came out of my mouth surprised me as well as the grocery vigilante. "Well, aren't you a nice man," I said, hardly able to believe my own words. "Hope you have a nice day."

He was flummoxed and did an about face that would have pleased the Naval Academy. And I just stood there, unable to believe that I had not scorched this jackass with the words he deserved. But obviously my lesson was not over, as my attention was drawn by a grackle that was making a huge commotion a few yards away. He was pecking away at something on the ground as though he had just discovered the ultimate grackle food. But it wasn't food at all, as I walked over to see what he was pecking. I couldn't believe it. It was a five-dollar bill, just lying there. Not an amount of money that would change my life. But somehow, it appeared that this grackle had been tapped to reward me for speaking the words from the peaceable kingdom that eludes us, just beyond the horizon, though we may be able to conjure it into being for just a moment. Perhaps the lowly oft despised grackle was the best messenger to set me straight on how the world works, beyond our ken.

Love Is Not Enough

Just loving you I thought was enough
I have loved all your creatures
Not just the beautiful ones but also
The strange and wily ones that
Slither away before I can touch them
The vultures that hiss at me from fenceposts
Before swooping down on the sad roadkills
Their angry bald heads refusing affection

Enchantment I've learned is the easy part
Anyone can laze in the shade of a great oak
But what happens when the bulldozers come
Or when the oak wilt fungus spreads like cancer
Or when the killing chemicals seep into the soil
Then the work begins of saving what we love

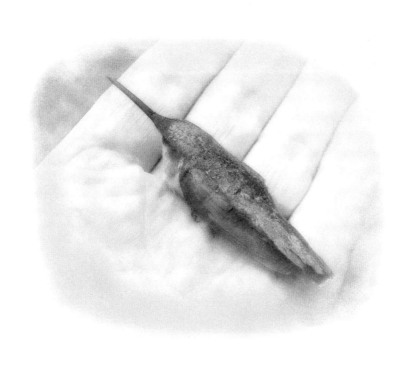

7

The Hummer on the Sidewalk

*I*f there are 13 ways of looking at a blackbird, as Wallace Stevens wrote, there must be many more ways to look at a hummingbird. Tiny but mighty, they migrate for long distances—up to 3,500 miles—and everything they do is amazingly fast. Their heart rates range as high as 1,260 beats per minute, and their wings beat at about 70 times per second in normal flight but can zoom up to 200 times per second during a high-speed dive. No wonder their flights are audible, making them sound something like bumblebees. They buzz like dive-bombers when competing for food, and you don't want to get in their way. And they are really fast eaters—their tongues zoom in and out of blossoms at the rate of 14 times a second.

Even more amazing to me are their iridescent colors, which I've learned come not from pigment but from the way the gridlike pattern of their feathers refracts light. The apparent color of any particular part of a feather depends upon the distance between its microscopic ridges. So when you say to yourself, admiringly, they are like little jewels, you are making both a poetic observation and an accurate comparison, since in fact their feathers do refract light like prisms.

Because they move so quickly, and they are always in motion, it's hard to get a bead on a hummingbird. But one day I got an unexpectedly intimate closeup. I was working in downtown Austin, and I came upon a ruby-throated hummingbird lying on the sidewalk, apparently dead. I thought he might have been stunned by slamming into a window, and so I carried him up to my office on the eighth floor and found a small box to put him in. I punched airholes and then wondered what on earth to do with him if he came to. And then I thought about all the flowers in Zilker Botanical Garden, just across Lake Austin, so I went to my car, box in hand, and drove to the garden.

I took the hummingbird out of the box and held him in the palm of my hand, almost not believing that I was holding something so dear and usually so elusive. It was like holding light or energy itself. I held my breath and watched in wonder as he began to stir. He walked to the end of my finger and perched there, looking around, his head moving back and forth. He must have thought he had awakened in paradise, surrounded by so many blossoms. His long tongue darted in and out a few times, like a kid in a candy store. His wings started beating, and he hovered for a moment, then zoomed away.

There are moments when, as Blake wrote, you are given the gift to "Hold infinity in the palm of your hand."

The Enigma of Beauty

Why are so many things more beautiful
Than they have to be in order to survive
Hummingbirds dive bombing each other
At the feeder dazzle with iridescent splendor
Is beauty in the eye of the human beholder
Who is viewing a bejeweled treasure in motion
Or in the eye of the courted assessing mate
Who perceives promise in such shining colors

As I was weeping in despair that summer day
At the castle in Italy I looked up and saw him
A tiny shimmering hummingbird drawing nectar
From a basket of red flowers and then I knew
As I drew inexplicable comfort from this little bird
That such beauty is a gift for all that we endure

8

A Butterfly Story
Part 1: Monarchs and the Mysteries of Migration

*M*any years ago, in the days when I wasn't afraid to drive alone in Mexico, I set out from the city of Morelia in a rental car with iffy tires in search of monarch butterflies gathering in their Mexican winter home. I drove along a narrow, winding road through the once volcanic region known as the Mil Cumbres (Thousand Peaks) to the tiny pueblito of Macheros, high in the remote reaches of Michoacán, not passing a single car on the way. I had arranged to meet a guide in Macheros, at the base of Cerro Pelón, or Bald Mountain, an imposing now-dormant volcano that is part of Michoacán's Transvolcanic Range.

At first, the dusty pueblito looked deserted and a little forlorn, but then I saw a vaquero in chaps leading two horses my way, one for each of us. The only way to reach the Cerro Pelón sanctuary, the most remote of five monarch sanctuaries scattered on mountaintops around this part of central Michoacán, is by horseback or by an arduous all-day hike on foot.

A small church marks the entrance to the path up to the sanctuary, which lies just below the peak. It was unusually bright and warm for a January day, but as we climbed, the temperature began to drop, and the skies turned gray. After nearly three hours of riding, we began to see butterflies fluttering here and there and alighting on wild salvia blossoms. Above 11,000 feet, the stands of cedar and Montezuma pine gave way to the cathedral-like oyamel firs that mark the core of the sanctuary. The firs are the favorite resting place for the millions of migrating monarchs that make their way over thousands of miles in late fall to these small patches of favored habitat. I could see, however, that many firs had been cut down, their rotting stumps a testament to the illegal logging that has endangered the sanctuaries.

As we approached the remaining stands of firs, their long, sloping branches were drooping with the weight of what I at first thought were thick clusters of autumn leaves. Shafts of sunlight began breaking through the clouds, and suddenly, the "leaves" cascaded from the branches. I could almost feel the breeze generated by hundreds of thousands of fluttering wings, as the monarchs wheeled aloft, filling the air overhead with tongues of flame. It was a Pentecost of butterflies. The strange crackling sound made from their collective fluttering is known as a susurrus, and I felt as though they were speaking in a kinetic language.

Overwhelmed by their collective grace, and breathless from the altitude, I sank down on a rock, and my eyes filled with tears of sheer wonder and astonishment. I had anticipated the beauty, but no one had told me about the otherworldly sound of so many wings in motion. A band of angels, if there were a multitude of them, would make a sound like that in flight, I thought, in my near delirium. I felt as though I had been baptized by butterflies, immersed.

I was glad I had worn black, as my clothing absorbed the heat of the sun, and I became a willing butterfly perch. I was soon covered with butterflies seeking warmth. As the monarchs sunned themselves on my sleeves and pant legs, I could see the silky fur of their thoraxes, and I wanted to reach out and touch them but didn't. The toll their epic journey had taken on some of them was apparent. Some bore wings that were badly tattered by the long flight from their summer homes to this place where they had never been before.

Monarchs have been known to fly as much as 265 miles a day on their journey south to Mexico, which can take them two months to complete. Some of them depart from as far north as Canada, a journey of as much as 5000 miles. There have been many theories proposed over the years for the mystery of monarch migration—of how the monarchs manage to navigate thousands of miles to these small patches of mountaintop, arriving around the first of November every year, on the Día de los Muertos, the Day of the Dead.

In Mexican legend, the monarchs are believed to be the souls of the dead, returning home for a visit. Many scientists, however, think the migration mystery was at least partly solved by an experiment by a German scientist that I consider both cruel and possibly flawed. While some experts had speculated that the monarchs use an inner "map" for navigation, a biologist named Henrik Mouritsen set out to prove that they simply use the sun to navigate and have no "map" per se. He displaced 72 monarchs from their homes in Canada more than 1600 miles to the west, enclosing them in a plastic container and tethering them to a pole, to find out if they would correct their heading on their migratory flight when released They didn't, and flew southwest, as they would have from their home, rather than southeast, as they would need to in order to reach Mexico from their new and strange takeoff point.

It seems obvious to me that all Mouritsen proved was that you can throw a monarch off course by scrambling its sensory data and placing it in alien conditions, rather like playing blind man's bluff. What Mouritsen didn't know, and what no one seems to know for sure, however, is how the monarchs actually home in on the tiny patches of ground where their ancestors wintered once they've headed in the right direction. If you say "instinct," you're just begging the question. As physicist David Bohm once told Einstein as they were arguing about quantum mechanics, there are too many hidden variables within the mystery to be satisfied with a static answer.

The saddest irony of all is that the lingering mysteries of the great monarch migration may not be solved before the migration continues to dwindle and perhaps finally end. Although Mexican authorities have cracked down on the illegal logging in the sanctuaries, the biggest threat to the migration lies in farming practices in the U.S. that have done away with huge swaths of the habitat that has traditionally sustained the monarchs on their way south. The milkweed plants that the butterflies feed on are disappearing at an alarming rate because of the use of herbicides. There is virtually no milkweed left in much of Midwestern farmland now.

And so we are in danger of losing one of the great wonders of the natural world. There will still be monarchs, but will they continue to make that astonishing journey that eludes our ability to understand? Will the souls of the dead still return to the fir branches on remote mountain-tops to bring a cosmic connection to the land of the living—to speak in their collective kinetic language, the language of a million wings?

Sequestered Sunday

Let's imagine we are on a vigil
Or even better a vision quest
Away from the usual comforts
That satisfy our many appetites

Let's allow ourselves to be hungry
For once and not sate ourselves
And let's see what we hunger for
Let's see what our souls are craving
What they've long been starving for

Could it be this quiet solitude
So quiet here I can hear the trees
Thinking out loud through their roots
So quiet I think I can hear wolves
Somewhere in the distance howling
At the moon that we can finally see
Waxing and waning in clear night skies

With no business as usual to interrupt
This new sacred communion we may drink
A heady new wine and break open the loaves
That miraculously multiply to fill us all

I watch the monarchs flutter down
Like tongues of flame of the Pentecost
Teaching us all the languages we need
To talk to the earth and to hear each other

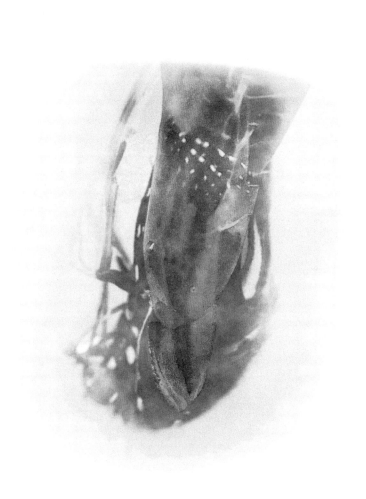

9

A Butterfly Story
Part 2: The Mysteries of Metamorphosis

Six months after my husband died in Guatemala, I saw an ad for a "healing center" in Costa Rica called Asclepios, named for the god of healing and medicine in ancient Greece. At the time, I was still operating almost completely from the right side of my brain—the side governed by emotion rather than reason—and on impulse, I bought a plane ticket and reserved a room. In my fuzzy, irrational state, I felt that Costa Rica would bring me close—but not too close—to the place where Gary died. I had already begun the journey that I had come to think of as a pilgrimage to deal with my grief, and I envisioned being cocooned in nature at Asclepios, not realizing how apt that image would become.

Two days after I arrived at the center, which was surrounded by green, mist-covered hills ideal for growing coffee and contemplating at dawn, I was still in the state of mind that I think of now as my partial zombie state—putting one foot in front of the other but not really alive. I was a harmless zombie, not seeking to feed on the flesh of the living, but I knew dimly that my eyes had a kind of dazed, unfocused look that must have been disconcerting to the young American women who had come to the center for massages and sunbathing by the pool.

Determined to keep in motion, I scheduled a day trip with Pedro Torres, the charming driver who had brought me from the airport in San José to the healing center. He had agreed to drive me to Poas Volcano and then to the nearby nature center at La Paz Waterfall. I was looking forward to toucans and butterflies and the sound of falling water.

"I have to warn you, said Pedro, as we set out. "The volcano is usually covered in mist. You can't always see it." As we wound our way up, I could see evidence of the 2009 earthquake that had killed hundreds in the area around the volcano. The main problem, said Pedro, was the mudslides that had covered roads, sent boulders down mountainsides and smothered people in their homes. "No one could get away," he said. "And then the roads were gone, so no one could get to them to help them."

And yet the scars were already disappearing. Green shoots were already springing up from the rubble, rewriting the script of loss on the landscape in a natural resilience I could only marvel at. Pedro said that most of the people who lost their houses and livelihoods had remained near the volcano. "No one wants to leave," he said. "This is home."

I had seen that stubborn resistance to giving up on a place time and again when I was growing up on the Gulf Coast. Most people, including my parents, cleaned up debris and repaired roofs after each hurricane, rebuilding their lives as though disaster would never happen again. "It's only material things," they would say. "What counts is that we survived."

In a sense, I supposed, being human has always meant living on the edge, one way or another—on a storm-ridden coast, in an earthquake zone, amid an epidemic, under a volcano, within a violent or besieged culture, near a battlefront or along a tornado alley—but the odds of staying safe seemed to be shifting. Losing Gary had made almost all ground I walked on feel unsafe.

We parked in a mostly vacant lot and then walked past a brilliant array of bromeliads lining the path to the volcano. The morning rain had left drops of water on their leaves that shimmered like tiny prisms. The earthquake had destroyed the park around the volcano, but the thirsty plants were already disguising the evidence of upheaval. As Pedro had warned, the mist was so heavy we couldn't actually see into the crater below, but there was a faint smell of sulfur in the air, and I could hear an ominous bubbling sound, as the volcano made itself known. The devil's brew, I thought.

I asked Pedro why there was so little evidence of indigenous culture in Costa Rica. He thought for a moment, then shrugged. "We only have about 100,000 indigenous left," he said. "They've all been pushed into little reserves, or they have become no different from other people. They are losing their languages." That sounded familiar, I said. I mentioned that my Choctaw ancestors had been forced to leave their land and travel the Trail of Tears, losing thousands of their numbers, while those who stayed behind had to hide out in the woods for nearly a century.

"Well, I'm half Chorotega," said Pedro, "but it's not something I talk about very much. The name Chorotega means 'the fleeing people.' We came here from Southern Mexico many centuries ago to keep from being slaves to the Mayan rulers. The Chorotega fought very hard against the Spanish when they invaded. They had the most organized resistance here of all the indigenous people. But of course you know what happened. And now most Chorotega people live in Guanacaste, up in the north."

"We'll all be the fleeing people," I said, "if global warming keeps up."

"Mother Earth has a fever," said Pedro, "and she's going to shake a few of us off." He suddenly smiled as he spied something glittering that was hidden in a crack on the railing where we had been leaning. It was a little gold heart that someone must have left behind as an offering to the volcano, but Pedro had a different idea. "This is for you," he said, handing me the heart. "I think the volcano wants you to have it." So perhaps the devil had decided to be kind, for once. I certainly had nothing worth trading for a heart of gold. My shriveled soul at the moment felt smaller than a grain of salt.

We waited in vain for the mist to clear and decided to head for the nature center, located on a flank of the volcano, even as it began to rain. "In a cloud forest, it's always raining," said Pedro. As we neared the nature center, the roads got worse. Rain was collecting in ruts and deep puddles in the road. "The epicenter of the earthquake was very close to here," he said. "They had to rescue hundreds of tourists from the area around the waterfall."

Despite the rutted roads, the La Paz nature center, which had been rebuilt, turned out to be something like a theme park, with an elaborate welcome center and a series of exhibits that included a jaguar in a cage, which made me cringe. But I was eager to see the butterfly observatory, which was regarded as one of the best in the world. As I walked into airy enclosure, I was surrounded by a cloud of fluttering blue morpho butterflies.

Along a display board hung a row of dangling cocoons from which blue wave butterflies were just beginning to emerge. Blue waves resemble the larger and more numerous blue morphos of the region, with the dorsal sides of their upper wings a bright neon blue patterned with white transversal bands and white spots. I watched as a newly emerged blue wave clung to its empty chrysalis and began to try out its wings, moving them tentatively back and forth, as though it were getting used to the idea of becoming airborne after crawling through the world as a worm.

After a few moments, the blue wave fluttered purposefully into the air, aiming toward the flowers and ripe fruit that had been set out as a first feast for the butterflies who now scorned the leaves of the euphorbia plants they had fed on as caterpillars.

Metamorphosis, I thought, is always a kind of miracle, though not without pain. As Ovid described it so many centuries ago in his masterwork of mythic stories, metamorphosis is not something that is chosen, but which seems to involve a shape-changing transition that appears drastic, but is somehow inevitable or appropriate—a fearful maiden escaping rape by becoming a tree, men becoming Circe's pigs that embody their base animal hungers.

A lowly caterpillar must endure a kind of death and dissolution in order to become transformed, to change from little more than a voracious eating tube into a delicate winged creature that drinks nectar through a straw. It's a mystery of transformation that scientists have only recently begun to solve, using 3D scans that allow them to see inside the chrysalis as the caterpillar dissolves into a kind of primordial genetic soup from the which the butterfly takes shape.

I wondered what it would feel like to emerge with wings from the prison-like dormancy of an earlier, earth-bound self. It was not an academic question, as I watched the newly hatched butterfly try out its wings. Butterflies have offered us a symbol and a promise that change is possible. I knew that out of Gary's death and the end of our life together, I would have to find a new life as a new being if I were going to survive. Somehow, I would have to grow wings.

Looking beyond my own bereavement, I wondered if humans were actually capable of transformation. Could we as humans change enough to make a sustainable world—could we transform ourselves from the stage of devouring everything in sight into a different state—one of sipping our resources from a straw and winging our way more lightly into the future?

All I knew then was that change was possible. And that is what I have held on to for dear life, just as the brand-new blue wave butterfly clung to its chrysalis as it spread its wings.

The New Extinction Math

How much is a butterfly worth
In the new zero-sum math

In which each species
Must prove it is worth saving

So what's the price tag, say,
On saving the Monarchs

Let's calculate the cost/benefit ratio
Of a Monarch vs. an undrilled oil well

Better still let's estimate the pain/payoff
That the new math will require us to use:

The Monarch doesn't generate revenue
They can't be taxed nor do they create jobs

They don't use any oil or gas
In their 3000 mile migration south

They extract no-cost nectar from milkweed
Along their path in the American Midwest

They pay no rent on the Oyamel fir trees
Where they winter on Michoacán mountaintops

The Mexicans say they carry the souls of the departed
For free when they arrive on the Day of the Dead

They charge no fees for us to watch them and listen
To the susurrus of millions of stained-glass wings

Okay I have done the math and the weight
Of a single Monarch wing equals the weight of a soul

So in the old math of intangible beauty and grace
Losing the Monarchs is a price beyond measure

10

Butterfly Story
Part 3: The Mysteries of Life and Death

*F*ive years after my husband's death, I traveled to the pyramids of Teotihuacán, north of Mexico City, for a spiritual retreat that was centered around Mexico's Día de los Muertos, or Day of the Dead, which coincides with Halloween and All Saints Day on the Anglo calendar. In Mexico, the Día de los Muertos is not a day of mourning or scary haunting but a bittersweet celebration of the dead, as though they awake from their eternal sleep for a day each year to enjoy a fiesta with loved ones. It is also the day that the monarch butterflies begin arriving from points north at their sanctuaries in the mountains of Michoacán, bringing with them, according to Mexican legend, the souls of the departed.

During the retreat, we spent our days at the pyramids and the evenings at a simple but beautiful lodge nearby called the Dreaming House, owned by a Toltec craftsman in whose family the land had been for generations. From the balcony in front of my room, I could see the top of the imposing Pyramid of the Sun, the world's third largest, and the occasional hot-air balloon transporting sightseers around the ruins of the mysterious civilization that has been compared to that of ancient Rome. We would be climbing the huge pyramid on the last day of the retreat, after working our way from the Pyramid of Quetzalcoatl, the mythic winged snake, through the plazas of earth, water, air and fire, to the Pyramid of the Moon. In each stage of our journey we would be facing our fears and sorrows and letting go of the things that didn't serve us.

On the afternoon of the 31st, in preparation for building our individual ofrendas, or altars, in honor of our departed loved ones, we took a bus to a small village known for its special Day of the Dead market, where vendors sold all manner of memento mori, including the usual sugar calaveras (skulls) and special bread called pan de muerto that local people favored. There were chocolate skulls, miniature caskets decorated like birthday cakes, and whimsical calacas (skeletons) in various lifelike poses. Children were roaming freely around the market, sampling the macabre sweets, and I wondered what it would be like to grow up in a culture where death and the dead were not something to be feared and avoided but accepted as a natural part of life.

Early that evening we prepared our ofrendas in a large room in the Dreaming House, and all of us contributed to a path of marigolds leading out to the street that would point out a way for the departed to find our altars. On my altar I placed a photo of my late husband Gary in one of his favorite Italian suits and added a pair of earphones that Gary had used with his iPhone, not just for the music but to quiet the tinnitus that had tormented him for years. I added a skeleton band of mariachi musicians, as we had both loved mariachi bands.

Many of us left our altars when we heard a parade passing by, and we joined in a festive group of children in costumes, their faces painted like calaveras, who were dancing down the street. They were celebrating the first part of the Day of the Dead, the Día de los Angelitos, commemorating departed children with a showing of high spirits and mischief.

We gradually trickled back to our altars, one by one, a process that would continue all night, as some wanted to keep vigil until dawn. For a time, I was alone in the room, and I lit a candle and sat, cross-legged, in front of the altar I had made for Gary, not shedding tears but aching with sadness and longing as I looked at his picture.

After a while, the picture seemed to waver and change, and I blinked my eyes as the image appeared to morph into a pyramid, with Gary's tie becoming a pathway to the top, where his smiling face gleamed over the pyramid like the sun. I supposed I was anticipating the next day, when we would be climbing the Pyramid of the Sun in the final ritual that we had been working up to all week. As I looked at the photographic image shimmering in candlelight on the altar I had built of memories and reminders, I had a sudden feeling that I would see Gary the next day at the top of the huge pyramid, however implausible that would be.

The next morning we began our journey at the partially restored structure known as the Palace of the Butterflies, where Toltec priests had lived and presided over the rites of initiation into the sacred mysteries of their civilization. The name Teotihuacán, I was reminded, has been translated as the place where humans become divine, and butterflies appear to have played a symbolic role in that transformation. Butterflies even appear on the shields of warriors.

We then gathered at the base of the Pyramid of the Sun to prepare for a climb that would be arduous for many. We made our way up the pyramid in stages, pausing at each level to circle in the pyramid in a meditative walk. When we reached the top, everyone gathered in a circle in a shared celebration of joy, but I quietly slipped away to the edge of the pyramid, where I sat down, feeling despondent and alone. Catching a movement from the corner of my eye, I saw a butterfly fluttering near me, and without thinking, I reached out my left hand, and the butterfly landed on my palm. It was not a monarch, I knew, as the monarchs would have begun arriving this very day at their sanctuaries far away in the mountains of Michoacán.

This was a rather plain patch butterfly, black with white spots and small smudges of orange, though I didn't know which of the various species of patch butterflies it was. It remained in my palm quietly for a moment and then began to move its wings slowly back and forth, back and forth. "Oh my God," said a startled friend who had sat down nearby, feeling overwhelmed by her own inner currents of grief. "Oh my God," she repeated, looking on in wonder as the butterfly continued to move its wings. Hundreds of thousands of wings, I had learned, make a susurrus, a sound like the heavens cracking open, but these wings were silent.

The little butterfly stayed there in my hand for several moments as my tears began to fall, and all time and all space seemed to collapse into the motion of its wings, which kept moving like the breath of the cosmos. Accept and give, accept and give. Life and death, death and life. Gary has never left you, said the wings. He is not here, yet he is here.

My butterfly journey, which had begun many years ago with a visit to the migratory monarchs in the sanctuary of Cerro Pelón, had come full circle with this ragged-looking lone emissary bringing me a message of improbable hope on this remote pinnacle atop a ruined civilization, reminding me of my everlasting connection to a wondrous and mysterious natural world where the souls of the departed return on the wings of butterflies.

And so for all of you who have lost a loved one or who have suffered a grievous wound, I wish you the gift of a butterfly fluttering in the path in front of you, bringing you the gift of connection to the living, breathing soul of the world. The gift is free.

Wonder Years

When do they end, the wonder years
Is it when we can no longer imagine
Fairies or guardian angels or Cheshire cats
Or when talking deer and flying elephants seem silly

The funny thing is that I still wonder
And find the world as much full of wonder
As when I believed that I could fly someday
And talk to dolphins and birds and horses

I wonder no less now at a hummingbird
And still find rainbows a miracle
And still cannot bear the death of an animal
Whether in a movie or in a book or for real

I still find myself talking to creatures
That I meet on a path or on the street
Saying hello to the roadrunners and deer
That stop for a moment before dashing away

I have long since lost illusions of bright horizons
As we willingly drill and pave the last wild places
But I refuse to let go of the enduring love
That I still find in flashes and glimmers

I greet butterflies and dragonflies as they alight
On flowers and sometimes on my hand
I think they bear glad tidings of connection
To a world still mysterious and grand

11

The White Shaman Dog of Teotihuacán

For many years I spent a week on retreat in late October, cul-
minating in the Day of the Dead, at Teotihuacán, the ancient
pyramid complex near Mexico City. Nearly every time I spent
there in the company of fellow seekers, something extraordinary would
happen. And so it was four years ago, on the day when we were to climb
the great Pyramid of the Sun, I got a call from the kennel where I had
boarded my dog Molly. She had gotten very sick, and they had taken
her to the nearby animal hospital. After running some tests, the vet had
concluded that her gallbladder had become so infected that it had to
be removed, or she would die. But the operation did not have a great
success rate, and chances are she would not survive.

I wept as I told them to go ahead with the operation. And I went
to sit in the shade near the pyramid, where the group had gathered before
climbing the pyramid, a solemn ritual. But as I sat on the grass and wept,
a beautiful white dog appeared and trotted over to me and climbed in
my lap. I was startled, as she licked the tears from my face, and I just
held her, despite warnings from my friends about various diseases she
might have. Eventually I got up to join the group as we ascended the
pyramid in stages.

When we reached the top, we gathered in a circle, and I looked
down to see that the dog had somehow followed us up, and she was
lying at my feet. I knelt and held her, just as I was being held in some
unfathomable and compassionate mystery. And when I got back to my
room, I learned that Molly had survived the operation. The mysterious
dog who licked my tears and followed me to the top of the pyramid became known as the white shaman dog. I looked for her when I returned
to Teo the next year, but I never saw her again.

For Molly: A Dog

When dogs made that devil's bargain
To come close to our fires
Seeking warmth and food in our caves
I wonder if they knew what it would cost them

When we touch a wolf in dog's clothing
And call a creature that knows its name
We touch a being that comes willingly
Sacrificing its freedom to join us

I think they came to us as emissaries
From the wild sent to remind us
Of our connection to creation
To fill the holes in our hearts

I think, too, they came to teach us of loss
To prepare us for grief and death
As their images crowd our altars
Before those of family and friends

There is no learning curve, however
For losing the loved ones in our lives
Nor is there such a thing as a little death
Because each one is part of the mystery

12

The Heron at the Shore

Two years after my husband died, I had settled with my extended family into a beach house at Gulf Shores, Alabama, for a Thanksgiving reunion. Holidays were hard for me, and Gary had always been with me for these annual gatherings at the shore. My dad would rent a large beach house somewhere on the shore between Mississippi and Florida, a stretch of sand and vacation houses that was sometimes called the Redneck Riviera. Everyone would pitch in to cook or shop, and it was a good way for our far-flung extended family to connect.

The beaches were blessedly empty during these cold days of late fall, and I escaped from the friendly clamor in the house for long walks, letting the wind and waves waft through my solitude. One day at sunset I was walking along the beach, feeling particularly lonely and bereft, when I saw a great blue heron standing in the shallow water. He was looking out to sea, as still as a statue. On impulse I took off my shoes and slowly waded out until I was standing beside him. He didn't even ruffle a feather.

We stood together for several moments, as I tried to be as utterly still as he was. The unflappable stillness of the bird, as the tide lapped against the shore, and his calm acceptance of my clumsy attempt at communion, soothed my aching, restless spirit. This happened again the next sunset and for several evenings until I had to leave. The last evening, when I went to say goodbye, he was gone, but he had left a feather on the shore where we had hung out together. I still have the feather as a reminder of my unlikely wading companion.

The Idea of Love at Troncones

At Troncones Beach a heron and an egret
Fish together every morning

One white one dark as the other's shadow
They are bonded by some force or another

As I watch them I wonder if this is love
Of a kind that binds us unknowingly

I once said I love all cats
Though I haven't met all the world's cats

I know that I love all horses
Because I've never met one I didn't

So then it's possible to love
The many through the one or two

So does that mean I can know
The ocean through a single wave

Or that I can love the forest
Through a single tree or even a leaf

For if that's so
May I love some and not all

May I single out a tree
A cat or a horse to love

And remain indifferent to all
Those who aren't my type

Can I embrace a vast galaxy
Through a lone bright star

Can I adore all rivers
Through a single ripple

Can I love all birds
Through one small sparrow

Can I cherish all insects
Through a solitary buzzing bee

For if that is so then each of us
Is a portal to love unbounded

And within each of us jostle
Horses, galaxies, rivers and oceans

13

The Swan Who Loved Me

I'm not sure how our strange love affair began, but I remember one day seeing a beautiful swan swimming past the fishing dock on the lake near my house where I went to meditate every morning after my husband's death. On impulse I retrieved Gary's old kayak that was still lodged in the rack beside the lake and borrowed a paddle lying nearby. I lugged the kayak to the water's edge and climbed in, feeling clumsy and out of shape, as I hadn't paddled in a long time, perhaps avoiding it because Gary had died in a kayak, though a long way away from our placid lake.

I paddled frantically upstream, trying to catch up to the swan, until I saw that he had stopped and appeared to be waiting. Though I had been warned that swans can be aggressive and can attack at any moment, I paddled up beside him. On impulse, I pulled out my iPhone from my pocket, and I was astonished when he began posing for me. He arched his neck and fluffed his tail feathers in what appeared to be a rather seductive way. I was bedazzled. I took picture after picture. I paddled back to the park and heaved the heavy kayak back onto the rack, marveling at the beautiful creature that seemed to have dropped randomly into my world.

The next morning, the swan appeared in the morning mist and swam up to the dock where I was standing, agog. He tried out an array of poses as I pulled out my iPhone, my hands almost shaking in disbelief. I spoke to him, telling him how beautiful he was, and he accepted my compliments as any regal being would. Over the next days, I began calling him Sweetie, the name I used to call my husband when I was feeling especially affectionate.

Sweetie did feel like something out of a myth, but this was not the story of Leda and the swan, with the hapless Leda overpowered by Zeus in the guise of a swan. It was simply one of those mysterious connections that fall into our lives like moments of grace and that don't bear a lot of looking into, but rather inspire grateful acceptance. I never knew when Sweetie would show up during my early mornings on the lake, but whenever he saw me, he would speed up to the dock and arch his neck in that seductive way. I never fed him, but I always complimented him. He would reply in gabbled swan speak. And this strange mutual courtship continued for the next three years or so until he stopped showing up, and I never saw him again.

Despite the nickname, I never felt that Sweetie was somehow embodying the spirit of my late husband. I don't think that's how these things happen. What I think is that I had lost my beloved partner, leaving me without masculine energy in my life, and this beautiful being showed up to fill that void. My husband's love, I felt, had dispersed into the universe, to be carried by the wind, the trees, and yes, the birds that surrounded me.

The River That Masquerades as a Lake

I think it must have been the Colorado
Masquerading as a slow-moving lake
That drew us to the old hippie neighborhood
Where you could still hear bands trying out
Some new songs on old drum sets in garages

We loved living just a stone's throw away
From our so-called lake which was actually
One of the series of big bulges in the coils
Of the snake that was the Colorado before
The dams tamed it into widened reservoirs

We would launch our kayaks from the little park
Where Bob the harbormaster would make wisecracks
About our dogs in their bright orange life vests
As he sat in his folding chair and cast a line
For the occasional perch that he always threw back

We'd paddle upstream to the narrow inlet
We pretended was a tributary of the Amazon
As we ducked under branches while turtles plopped
Into the murky water and great blue herons squawked
As they soared reluctantly from their wading spots

I never held it against the Colorado that another river
That rushed through a narrow jungle canyon in Guatemala
Claimed my husband as he spun from his red kayak
Into the rocky depths not far from the ruins of Tikal
As rivers don't pick and choose or play favorites

It was beside the Colorado aka Lake Austin that
The neighborhood musicians joined Marcia Ball
Who had brought her own portable piano to play
For a jazz funeral as we danced with parasols down
To the river and released rose petals into the current

And now every morning I walk down to the river that
Masquerades as a lake and I sit on the new fishing pier
To watch the sunrise as my little dog barks at the swan
I call Sweetie that swims up to me to say hello
While the great blue herons soar up from the opposite bank

14

Roadie the Roadrunner

*O*f Sweetie the swan had glided into my life, the roadrunner I called Roadie came running. He was a greater roadrunner with the distinctive iridescent blue and orange patch of skin behind each eye and a crest that he raised and lowered, depending on his mood. I can't remember when I first saw him, but it must have been in a blur. All of a sudden he was there, a presence in my yard. Usually he'd be on his way somewhere, but when I called to him, he'd come running and stop somewhere close and begin preening. He would raise his crest inquisitively when I spoke to him and sometimes puff out the feathers on his chest.

Roadie had a sort of proprietary air about him, as though my yard was definitely his territory. I enjoyed his company, however fleeting, without thinking too much about it. But Roadie seemed to know, as Sweetie did, that I could use a masculine presence in my life. One day, when roofers came to repair my roof, Roadie flew up and patrolled the roof, keeping a watchful eye on the workmen. They remarked on his keen attention to what they were doing.

Greater roadrunners make a variety of sounds, including odd clacking noises. But one day while standing on my back deck I heard a strange cooing noise coming from the back yard, getting closer. Coo-coo-coo. And as I was standing there, Roadie jumped up on the railing, continuing the cooing that I had never heard before. He then jumped down to a spot just in front of my feet and began performing what I finally realized was a kind of mating dance. When I didn't respond in kind, he eventually flew off.

I suppose Roadie realized he might need to impress me with his ability to provide because one day, when I was working on my computer out on the deck, he jumped up on the table right in front of me with a big toad in his mouth. He was flaunting it like a big steak dinner. Hey, check this out, he was saying in roadrunner speak. Again, when I didn't respond in a lady roadrunner way, he shook his head and flew off, perhaps seeking a more appreciative audience.

Eventually Roadie returned with a more appropriate mate, and they made a nest in the thick bushes across the road from my house. The lady roadrunner, I'm happy to note, is just as fast as he is. And just as charismatic.

The Language of Birds

How would I know it was a miracle
If your song hadn't come on
When the geese were flying

How could I hear you
Except through the radio
Or strangely in my dreams

You were not one for flowers
Or even so much for butterflies
But they do speak to me

It's not water into wine
Or sight restored to the blind
Yet it is a new kind of sensing

And what about that roadrunner
Who guards the house
And courted me one day

And who's to say the swan
Who swims to me so eagerly
In the misty morning isn't you

In your many new guises
I am surprised and awakened
By words made of light and wings

15

The Baby Bird at Chartres

T he coincidences began with the feathers I kept finding in my path, the first one a lone brown feather lying on the passenger seat of my car, the second a striped woodpecker feather lying near my doorstep on the morning I left for Paris, the next a gray pigeon feather I nearly stepped on as I left my table after having coffee at the Deux Magots before taking the train to Chartres for a week-long retreat. And there were more as the journey continued. Just feathers, right?

One afternoon in Chartres, I was being interviewed for a video presentation about my book *Written in Water: A Memoir of Love, Death and Mystery*, about my pilgrimage of healing following the sudden death of my husband. The book contains many passages about the role of birds in my journey, and I wanted to stress that I came to realize that what I was seeking was not just healing for myself, but for the natural world, and for all the species of birds, animals and plants that had become endangered during the Anthropocene era, the era of human domination of the planet. I came to this realization when I wrote an article about the endangered whooping cranes, who had become for me the canaries in the mine.

As I recalled that story, I told Claire, the interviewer, that I was reminded of that old gospel song "His Eye is on the Sparrow," which was inspired by the words of Jesus about birds in the gospel of Matthew. I tried to quote the passage, but I kept flubbing it. I must have repeated the words four or five times until I got it right: "Not one of them shall fall on the ground without your Heavenly father." But the words for the song should be "our eyes" on the sparrow, I added, because we are the ones who are called to help. "Not one bird shall fall," I repeated.

That night, a baby robin fell from its nest in a tree in the parking lot in front of the St. Yves residence next to Chartres Cathedral, and its agitated calling and that of its mother woke one of the members of the retreat group. Seeing that a cat was eyeing the baby bird, she placed the bird in a shoebox and brought to the meditation group the next morning, the last of the week, where it was decided that we should try to return the bird to the nest.

A ladder was secured, and the tallest man in the group climbed the ladder but was unable to reach the nest. "I can climb the tree," I said, even though it had been a very long time since I had climbed a tree. And so I did, slowly, branch by branch, reaching down as one of the men climbed the ladder and carefully reached up and placed the bird in my outstretched hand.

The baby was warm and soft in my hand, as it stirred gently and peeped. I cradled it and reached up toward the nest, stretching with all my might, fearful that I would fall short. Holding on to a branch with the other hand, I swung my way up, wishing I was a monkey. I felt the edge of the nest and dropped the baby safely inside, to the sound of cheers from my friends and the shedding of tears all round.

And so it was that our eyes were on the robin. Not one bird shall fall...

Calling for a New Kind of Song

There was a time that nature touched us
In the way of a teacher or a lover
And poets could sing blithely of her wonders

When Shelley saw a skylark in a cloud of fire
Keats heard the song of the nightingale and
Wordsworth wandered lonely as a cloud

But it was Yeats who looked beyond the swans
To the widening gyre and told us of rough beasts
Approaching and that the center could not hold

So what are we to do when we behold a tree
That beckons us to come close and then
Whispers in our ears please help me

We want to just let go of everything
So we can hold the wounded bird
And hear a new kind of song

We want to step into a river that is dying
And hear the murmurs from the current
That says we can't step twice in her waters

So we enter into a new kind of relationship
With the once wild world that needs us
As much as we have always needed her

So we listen, we listen, we listen
And in the silence we forge a bond
As we vow to never let go, never let go

16

The Spanish Dagger and the Willow

D o you talk to your plants? Or more importantly, do they talk back? Like all gardeners, I love my plants. I might even love them too much. But because I live in Austin, one of the most frustrating places to garden, I try not to get too attached to them because I know I might lose them—to hungry deer, to drought, to endless plus-100-degree-days, to flash floods, to baked caliche soil, to late or early freezes. And lately, I've lost beloved oaks to oak wilt.

Loving an annual can be a particularly fleeting affair, but even perennials can't promise to stay with you forever. Unusually cold winters can be particularly hard for plant lovers, who have to say goodbye to some long-term relationships. These days I lean toward cacti, the toughest customers in the plant world, who reward getting too close with a stab or a prickle. I might be a tree hugger, but I don't hug my cacti. But sometimes, I was to learn, they lean towards me.

And yes, of course I talk to my plants, even the prickly ones, and I was talking to them even before the bestselling book The Secret Life of Plants changed the way people—at least some people—looked at plants. Authors Peter Tompkins and Christopher Bird described the experiments by Cleve Backster, the former CIA polygraph expert, who decided on a whim to hook up his machine to plants and discovered that they reacted to all kinds of things, including the torture and dismemberment of their fellow plants.

Michael Pollan's superb piece about plants in *The New Yorker* described how scientists have found all kinds of ways to debunk Backster's experiment and to deny that plants actually have intelligence

Some researchers, however, who are thick-skinned pioneers in the new field of plant neurobiology, have argued that the sophisticated behaviors observed in plants, responding to complex environmental variables, from light, water, gravity, temperature, and soil components to toxins, insects and chemical signals from other plants, mean that there must be some kind of "information-processing system" in plants that is homologous to that in animals. And scientists familiar with the way computer systems work have suggested that plants may have a kind of "distributed" intelligence rather than a central "brain." They could, in fact, have an intelligence that may offer us some interesting possibilities.

Maybe you've had your own experiences with plants that seem to act or react in ways that indicate some kind of interaction with you. I have, though I know that plants don't "think" or "talk" in words. They speak by the way they grow, by thriving or withering, by moving toward sunlight, by ducking towards shade, by sending signals through their root systems, by using fungi as a "medium" for communicating to other plants—a kind of botanical wireless.

The two significant "conversations" I've had with plants involve a Spanish dagger and a golden willow, both of which were in trouble and needed help. One summer in Austin, the top-heavy Spanish dagger in my front yard was apparently in danger of toppling over, which I didn't notice until one day, as I was leaning over to fiddle with another plant beside it, the ten-foot tall plant ever so slowly, ever so gently, began to lean and then fall until its trunk was resting on my shoulder, leaving the razor-sharp blades safely away from my face. It was though someone had touched me on the shoulder to get my attention.

The golden willow was a different story in a different state. While I was living in Vermont back in the 1980s, I planted a small golden willow next to the babbling brook that ran in front of my house. Being so close to water, I assumed the willow would thrive, and it did briefly until it was attacked by aphids, which clung to its leaves and busily began to eat away. I was determined not to use pesticide, so I started with soap to get at the aphids, but it wasn't doing the job, so I simply began to strip the aphids off the leaves by hand, spending hours scouring them away. This went on for days until finally the pests didn't come back. And so I was relieved when I returned from a lengthy trip to see that the willow had grown, and its branches were drooping gracefully with beautiful green-golden leaves. It was a still day, with no wind, and I walked over to the willow to say hello. As I approached it, the branches quivered, and the leaves seemed to whisper something. I think it was saying hello. And maybe thanks.

Okay, I know I may be engaging in what literary critics would call a "pathetic fallacy," which means to attribute human characteristics or emotions to objects or aspects of nature—Wordsworth's "lonely as a cloud" being a prime example. But what I think is that the wind is the breath that gives a tree a voice and that its leaves speak in tongues that some of us can hear. They speak the mother tongue, as my friend Will Taegel of the Earth Tribe would say.

Trees That Talk in Tears

There is a tree I sit under sometimes
Because it offers shade on a hot day
But also because I feel peaceful there
All I have to do is sit down and it comes
This state of mind I don't feel elsewhere

One afternoon I was sitting there when
I felt some drops of moisture land lightly
On my forehead and I looked up surprised
To see just the bright sun and blue sky
And just a few thin shreds of clouds above

So where did these drops come from
If not from the bright blue sky
And I thought perhaps the leaves
Of the tree had been forced by the wind
To give up the moisture they had hoarded

But what if the tree "thought" perhaps
I was thirsty or needed the water
And let its leaves willingly give it up
Or even getting crazier about it
I wondered if trees could shed tears

Could this tree possibly be my friend?
Is it possible it enjoys my company?
Could the tree be sad or having a bad day?
Perhaps it was hinting that it was thirsty
So I brought the hose over to give it a drink

I would like to learn the language of trees
That talk to each other through their roots
Though my roots stop at the ground but
I do trace my ancestry as a kind of tree
So perhaps we have that at least in common

Most of the language of trees aims at each other
Deep underground where there is much
Intimacy and generous sharing of resources
But what if, what if, what if, what if, what if
This blessed tree is trying to learn my language

And those drops falling from its leaves
Are a kind of Morse code, drip, drip pause
Are you there it is asking are you there
For me when I need you because there
Will be times when we will need each other

17

The Dragon of Loneliness

*Y*ou could say that I have a thing for dragons, a kind of love/fear thing. With their ability to fly and to breathe fire, they represent for me the power of imagination—but also the deep potential for anger, vengeance and destruction we carry within us. I like to think of the oldest part of our brain, the amygdala, sometimes known as the lizard brain, as our inner dragon. The amygdala controls our most basic emotional fight-or-flight responses, instilling fear or urging us to take aggressive action. Breathe fire or fly away.

They could have filmed *How to Train Your Dragon* 1 and 2 in my writing studio. I don't have a Night Fury like Toothless or a Deadly Nadder like Stormfly. But if you look around my studio, you'll see lots of dragons on the wall and hanging from the ceiling: A sinuous plastic dragon from Hong Kong, a stylish balsa wood dragon I bought in Lisbon, an antique cloth dragon from San Francisco, a dragon calendar from Tibet. I also have a treasured 18th century Japanese scroll with a rather scary dragon depicted in ink.

But my favorite dragon is this little stuffed guy that I bought a few years ago at a toy shop on the Piazza Navona around Christmas. I was working on a book while at the American Academy in Rome, feeling very very lucky to be there. But unexpectedly I was overcome with loneliness as I looked out my window atop Janiculum Hill on the splendors of Rome. My late husband and I had treasured our time together in Italy, and I was finishing a memoir about his death and my pilgrimage through grief, which obviously triggered my sense of loss. But somehow what I was up against was even more primal than that. I felt that perhaps my real purpose in coming to Rome was to face what I came to call the dragon of existential loneliness.

It was during one of my long walks, winding up in the Piazza Navona, which was particularly festive on the days leading up to the Epiphany, that I saw this little dragon in the window of the shop called Sogni (Dreams). I bought it on impulse, not really knowing why I wanted it. Maybe it was a way of taming my dragon of loneliness, by making it small and cute. Once it was perched on my writing table, I began to feel better, and I felt my imagination beginning to get stronger than my fear. I wound up buying a small unicorn I noticed in the window of yet another toy shop to keep the dragon company as I worked. And as though I had entered some kind of magic kingdom, a double rainbow appeared outside my window on my last day in Rome.

As I prepared to leave, I packed the small dragon in my carry-on bag, and when I boarded my plane, I placed it in the overhead bin and settled into my seat. Before I had buckled my seatbelt, a woman and child came down the aisle and sat in the seats in the aisle across from me. The young boy was clearly autistic, and he really didn't want to be on the plane. After takeoff, he began to scream bloody murder, and passengers around him were alarmed. The stewardess arrived and asked the mother to do something, but the screaming continued.

For some reason, I thought of the dragon in my carry-on, and I stood up and retrieved it from the overhead bin. I began to make it fly in front of the boy, zooming it back and forth, back and forth. He began to watch it, mesmerized, and he stopped screaming. I held it out to him to hold it, but he stammered, "No dragon, no dragon." But then he reached out his arms to me. I held out the dragon to him again, but he shook his head. It wasn't the dragon he wanted.

I somehow found the boy's arms around my neck, and then I was holding him. I rocked him back and forth, and he rested his head on my shoulder for a few minutes. I set him down, and he took my hand, and we walked up and down the aisle for a while and then came back to his seat. He sat down and was quiet for the rest of the trip.

For a time, I didn't really know what to make of what happened. But I now think that the dragon of loneliness wound up connecting me in a primal way to the little boy, in the place where his—and my—deepest fears were found. The dragon flew through the barriers separating us and brought us together for a moment or two in what I can only call love.

And so for me, dragons represent the difficult things about ourselves that we have to stop running from and face someday, in one way or another—either to do battle with them or to make peace with them. And even to embrace them. Perhaps it's the dragons that do the training. We're the ones who need the lessons, right?

Calling Him by His True Name

My warrior vowed he would slay the dragon,
And I thought it was for me he fought
As I watched the clash from the castle window,
Wondering what our fate would be,
Until one day he faltered and fell,
Leaving me with his sword and shield.
And so I took them up despite their weight.

As sure as the sun came the dragon
Flying on fire in the morning light.
As I raised my shield and closed my eyes
I found that I was not burned
And that I was not afraid.
I looked up to see that his bright green eyes
Were gleaming like jewels and glistened like tears.

He asked in a voice of smoke
If he could tell me his secret name.
Yes, I said. I want to know.
My name is Loneliness, he said.
I can't be conquered by the sword.
If you will ride on my back and whisper my name
I will take you to see the world.

18

The Wind Horse and the Mountain Snake

A few years ago, I found myself living out a longtime dream, riding a feisty little Mongolian horse across vast, rolling green steppes that seemed to stretch out to eternity. Mongolians don't actually name their horses, but instead refer to them by one of their multiple words for shades of brown. Despite the tradition, I had come up with a name for my burnished brown horse with knowing eyes, tricky moves and a rock-star mane: James Brown. As it turned out, he more than lived up to his name, as I began to tune in to his unpredictable rhythms and lightning bursts of speed.

On this cool, bright summer day we were making our way to set up camp beneath a sacred mountain known as Mount Mandal. I was eager to make the trek up the mountain, where it was said you could communicate with your ancestors and with beloved ones who had departed. I had brought along my Native American flute, as I hoped to bring music to Mongolia from my Native American ancestors and to dedicate a song to my late husband.

I knew, however, as I watched the rest of the very fit group, most of them half my age, heading up the mountain on foot ahead of me, this would be a hard climb. I was still being affected by the altitude, and I trudged and huffed and puffed up to a rock promontory, where I stopped, exhausted, and caught my breath so I could play my flute. I had learned about the concept of the "wind horse" from a sage Buddhist monk we had met at a monastery earlier in the trip. We each have some "wind horse" power inside of us, he said, and its inner strength is a gauge of our life force. Right then, my wind horse felt very weak.

As I picked up my flute, I felt some strength and breath returning, and as I played, the notes seemed to waft up the mountain and through the valley below. I did have a fleeting vision of my late husband, floating toward me on a red kayak, here on this sacred mountain said to be full of ancestral spirits, and others told me later they could hear the music from high above me on the mountaintop.

I gathered myself for the ascent to the top, step by step, but when I reached the loose rocks near the top, I kept slipping and sliding, and it seemed to take forever to get there. The descent, I hoped, would be easier. But I was so exhausted, I just gave up dignity and slid down on my ass until the slope was easier and I could walk down. Then I began almost to run down the slope in sheer relief.

For some unknown reason, as I was picking up momentum, I paused suddenly, suspending my right foot in the air, like something out of a cartoon. It was as though I had frozen in place and couldn't move. Over to the right, I could see the rock where I had played the flute. But as I looked down where I was about to place my foot, there was a coiled snake, probably about four or five feet long, though to me he might as well have been ten feet. Being from Texas, I knew how to determine if a snake is poisonous by the triangular head, and this one clearly meant business.

All this cogitating on risk was instantaneous, and I was back up the slope in a blur. I later learned from the markings of the snake that it was a pit viper, which could have killed me. The Mongolian horse handlers later told me that my encounter with the snake was an encounter with the spirit of the mountain, which I might have awakened with my flute, and that it had given me a powerful blessing and protected me.

The next day, when we met with a local shaman, I noted that his robe was decorated with the skins of pit vipers. I recognized the pattern of dark bands on pinkish skin immediately. And so it was that I was later given the Indian name of Mountain Snake Woman.

Ode to a Mongolian Horse

You were my spirited steed
And I called you James Brown
Because of your soulful slick moves
And your glistening brown coat
And so we danced together
Getting to know our rhythms

On your back I have crossed rivers
I have circled the tattered ovoo
I have galloped over the steppes
Past the larches and wild asters
To the sacred mountain
As eagles soared overhead

I have drunk the magic mare's milk
Just as you drank the milk of your mother
Growing strong and fast
And so we are linked by airag
And by the tall grass
That nourished your mother

I would like to sing to you
In the Mongolian way
Saying Gingo-o-o-o
Let's go and conquer the world
Just as your ancestors
Carried the warriors to victory

So how can I say *bayartai* to you
I think of Anka singing
To her ailing animals
And making them cry
And it is hard for me
To hold back my own tears

I will take you home with me in my dreams
And at night I will place on you
Your khadsaar made of silver
You need no tashuur,
No whip for urging
And we will fly across the planet

Setting the sky ablaze
With your hoofprints at dawn
Back to your beloved Mongolia
To the endless green pasture
Where you belong
And where I long to be

19

The Deer's Cry
When Darkness and Light Come to Your Door

About a month before my husband's death in Guatemala, I saw a tiny newborn fawn in my backyard. It wasn't the first fawn to be born there, as the whitetail deer population in my neighborhood was expanding. But as I looked closer at the tiny creature, still learning clumsily how to walk, I thought what I was seeing must have been a trick of the light. The deer was solid black, from ears to hooves. I named the deer Issa, the Choctaw word for deer.

She was a melanistic deer, I learned, a genetic variation even more rare than albino deer. I didn't think of her arrival at the time as an omen, but simply as a beautiful variation from the norm. But after Gary's death, as I looked back at the weeks before I got the fateful phone call telling me of his death, I realized that Issa had been part of a kind of a natural early warning system that included a barred owl that kept getting closer and closer until he appeared on the back deck in the moonlight the night before Gary left for Guatemala. Nature, I felt, was bending towards me, not to stop the oncoming disaster but to prepare me for what was to come.

I was reminded of a black swan that appeared on the lake three years earlier. The swan was alone, and she was calling plaintively as she swam upstream. As it happened, Gary and I had been reading philosopher Nassim Nicholas Taleb's provocative book titled *The Black Swan: The Impact of the Highly Improbable*, which is about the illusion of certainty that comes with predictable events. For Taleb, the world is actually most changed by "black swan events," by which he meant unique, unpredictable outcomes of accidents and luck and seemingly freakish events.

The afternoon after we saw the swan, Gary told his dear friend Elspeth Rostow, who was still teaching at age 90 at the LBJ School along with Gary, about the swan we had seen and what a strong impression it had left on us. And just two days later, Elspeth died suddenly. In his grief, Gary recalled the rare and improbable swan and connected the appearance of the swan with losing Elspeth. He wrote a letter to several of our friends, saying that when we heard the news that Elspeth had passed away, "we knew that the black swan had been an omen that we didn't recognize—except that I was given the opportunity to tell Elspeth about it, just before her death."

Gary wrote that he "immediately thought about the richness of the image: grace, rarity, a regal quality, and of course the portent of the color. The black swan on the lake was alone, as swans usually are not. I'm not a believer in omens or signs, but this was one that could not be ignored. In retrospect, it seems both eerie and perfectly natural at the same time."

And perhaps the appearance of Issa had also been both eerie and perfectly natural at the same time. A black deer event rather than a black swan event. I saw Issa a few times after Gary's death and then she seemed to disappear. I never saw her again. I learned that she had been found by the side of the road, struck by a car, probably in the dark, with the driver unable to see her.

Ten years after Gary's death, I again thought I was seeing things. As I was walking in my neighborhood, I saw a small black deer in a yard just down the street from me. I had the impression that this young deer, who was grazing with a small herd of ordinary does, was female. A month later, the black deer was drinking from the birdbath in my backyard.

I told myself that the deer was not an omen or a warning. But just before Christmas, my father, aged 96, had a heart attack, and I thought, of course, of the deer. He told me once that he had never seen a black deer, despite his long association with the whitetail deer on his land in the Hill Country, for which he had become a fierce protector. On the night before he was to undergo a risky surgical operation, I dreamed of a deer, though this time it was not a black deer, but an enormous radiant white stag that dropped into the dream as a kind of photo bomb, clearly an icon. Even while I was dreaming, I knew this was no ordinary deer. For Native Americans, a vision of a white deer symbolizes a visitation from the Great Spirit, a message to be pondered, which I thought was fitting, since my Dad is part Choctaw.

The next day, shortly after the doctor informed us that my dad had come through the surgery safely, I looked down at my iPhone as something popped up on the screen. It was a video of an Irish singer performing the haunting melody, "The Deer's Cry," which was said to come from St. Patrick as an anthem of faith and protection. "I arise today," it begins.

The next morning I played the song on my iPhone for my Dad as he was sitting up in a chair beside his hospital bed, looking much as he always did, before his heart attack. He thought for a moment and said, "I know what the title should be for your next book: 'I Heard the Deer Cry.'" And as my own tears were welling up, he opened the title page of the John Grisham novel he had been reading and began to write something on one of the pages.

This is what he wrote:

> *I didn't know when*
> *I didn't know why*
> *But I knew it would happen:*
> *The day I heard the deer cry.*

I think he must have known that the deer, black and white, were not through with us. When Texas was paralyzed not long afterward by the polar vortex, and everyone had reverted to living in the dark ages, without power or running water, I couldn't help but wonder if this was another black deer event, a sudden and freakish happening when everything changes. For days I was confined to my house, surrounded by snow and icy roads. Most of my neighbors were without power or water and were shivering. The state froze to a halt.

And sure enough, one morning in the middle of *Snowvid*, as the once-in-a-lifetime event was called, I went to my front door and looked out to see the black deer right there in front of the door, looking in at me. She was a dark shadow in comparison to the glistening white snow that covered the walkway and the yard beyond. She did not flinch or run away when she saw me looking back at her, but almost seemed to be trying to talk, as a friend noted from the video I took of our encounter. Another friend remarked, "She loves you." But I don't think of it so much as love as simply connection. She appeared to be delivering a message.

And what was the message this time, except that the unexpected will always surprise you. And that it is not to be feared. When I was finally able to get to my doctor's appointment in town, I learned that I had been harboring a lump in my breast. As I began treatment over the next weeks, I knew that the deer had come to tell me that darkness is a part of life. And that the shadows may cast their own kind of light.

How Can Love Become Manifest

There are times when I look at birds
With what I think is simply love
But how will they know I love them
I try in vain to imitate their calls
How will I know they have heard me
When all I can offer is paltry seeds

And as for the black deer who comes
To my door looking in at me puzzled
And maybe wanting to come inside
I can tell her in words that I love her
But how in her world in her lexicon
Can she hear me from heart to heart

I can offer cracked corn as an offering
But it is inadequate to want I want to give
I want my love to warm her in the cold
But I cannot end the storms that rage
Nor can I melt the ice covering the green
That sustains her and her tan siblings

And so it is when I offer a prayer
How can I be sure it will arrive safely
As I am sending this prayer like smoke
That I hope will rise and reach the ears
That are tuned to every vibration on earth
And that will translate words into spirit

Made in the USA
Middletown, DE
07 October 2021

49810108R00069